To Dear Margaret & John,

A little something of

Australian Animals

Enjoy

Much Love +

Friendship

Mary & Louise xxxx

Feb 2004.

SILLY GALAH!

Omnibus Books
52 Fullarton Road, Norwood SA 5067
an imprint of Scholastic Australia Pty Ltd (ABN 11 000 614 577)
PO Box 579, Gosford NSW 2250.
www.scholastic.com.au

Part of the Scholastic Group
Sydney · Auckland · New York · Toronto · London · Mexico City ·
New Delhi · Hong Kong

First published in 2001.
Reprinted in 2002.
Text copyright © Janeen Brian, 2001.
Illustrations copyright © Cheryll Johns, 2001.

National Library of Australia Cataloguing-in-Publication entry
Brian, Janeen, 1948–
Silly galah!.
ISBN 1 86291 442 7.
1. Animals – Australia – Juvenile poetry. I. Johns, Cheryll, 1971–   . II. Title.
A821.3

Cheryll Johns used acrylic paint for the illustrations in this book.
Typeset in 23/25 pt Litterbox by Clinton Ellicott, Adelaide.
Printed and bound by Tien Wah Press (Pte) Ltd.

10 9 8 7 6 5 4 3 2   2 3 4 5 / 0

SILLY GALAH!

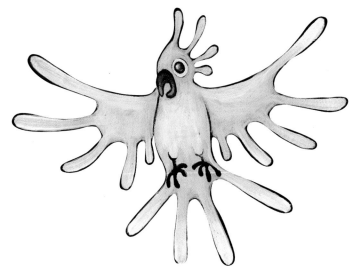

Janeen Brian

Illustrated by Cheryll Johns

An Omnibus book from Scholastic Australia

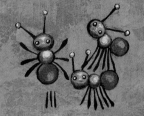

Echidna

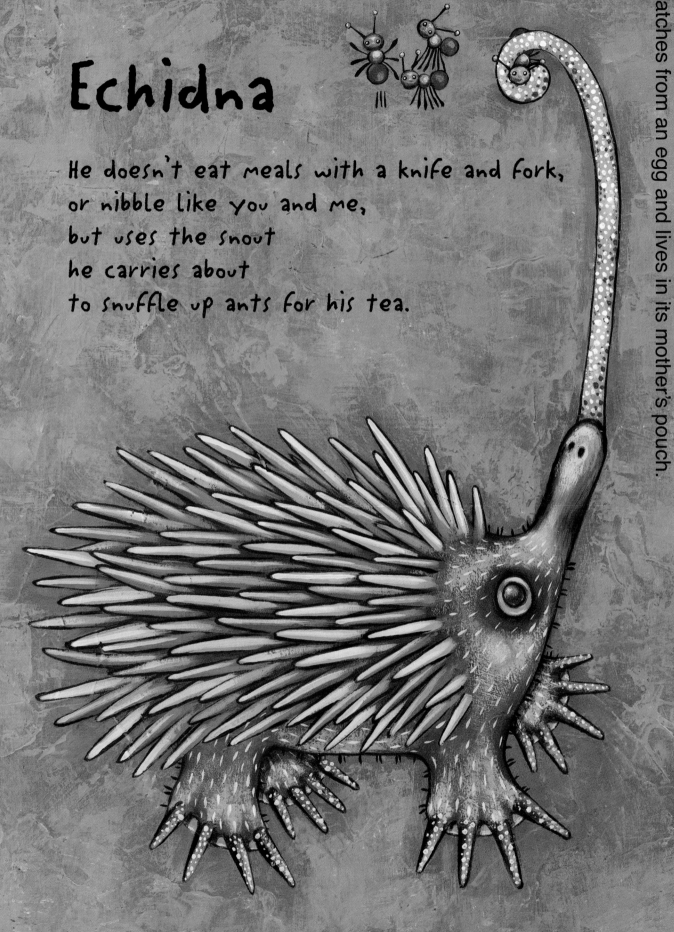

He doesn't eat meals with a knife and fork,
or nibble like you and me,
but uses the snout
he carries about
to snuffle up ants for his tea.

The echidna uses its long sticky tongue to catch its food – ants and termites. If danger is about,

hatches from an egg and lives in its mother's pouch.

Crocodile

Crocodile waits on the river bank,
watching creatures like me and you.
It's not out of respect —
it's just that he's checked
if we look like one mouthful or two.

eople, cattle and horses. Crocodiles swish their strong tails to swim. Webbed feet help them walk on boggy ground. Crocodiles live for a long time. They are related to dinosaurs.

are very bossy. They swoop on animals or people who come near.

Magpies have a clear, tuneful song. Sometimes they sing together. At nesting time, magpies

Magpie

Magpies strut around like kings
in black-and-white feathery
suits.
Their manner and song
are both loud and strong.
They're such Aussie bossy-boots!

Possum

The ringtail possum is fond of her tail,
which is curly and whirly and strong.
She swings, if she pleases,
among leafy treeses,
for berries and fruit all night long.

Cockatoo

When cockatoos gather round to chat,
up close or out in a clearing,
they set themselves down,
nod to others around,
then screech like they're all
    hard of hearing.

The cockatoo is a big bird with a strong, hooked beak. Cockatoos are noisy birds, but they are clever.

Sea-lions live and feed in water. They have their babies on land

Sea-lion

See the slithery sea-lion —
her body's kind of flippery.
She catches dinner in her mouth
'cause fish are kind of slippery.

Tree frogs eat insects, worms and lizards. They have special pads on their hands and feet for climbing.

Tree frog

Tree frog green
like shiny jelly,
hasn't got a button
on his little frog belly.

Koalas carry their babies in a pouch. When the babies are older, they ride on their mother's back. Koalas are fussy about the type of eucalyptus leaves they eat.

Koala

In the treetops high above,
koala quietly snoozes.
She picks a bunch
of leaves for lunch,
then settles back and chewses.

Kookaburra

He's the bird you can't ignore
on plains or bushland hilly —
for he's the one
just out for fun
who laughs himself quite silly.

heir food. They eat insects, snakes, frogs and other small animals.

Kookaburras lay their eggs in nests that they make in termite mounds, trees or buildings.

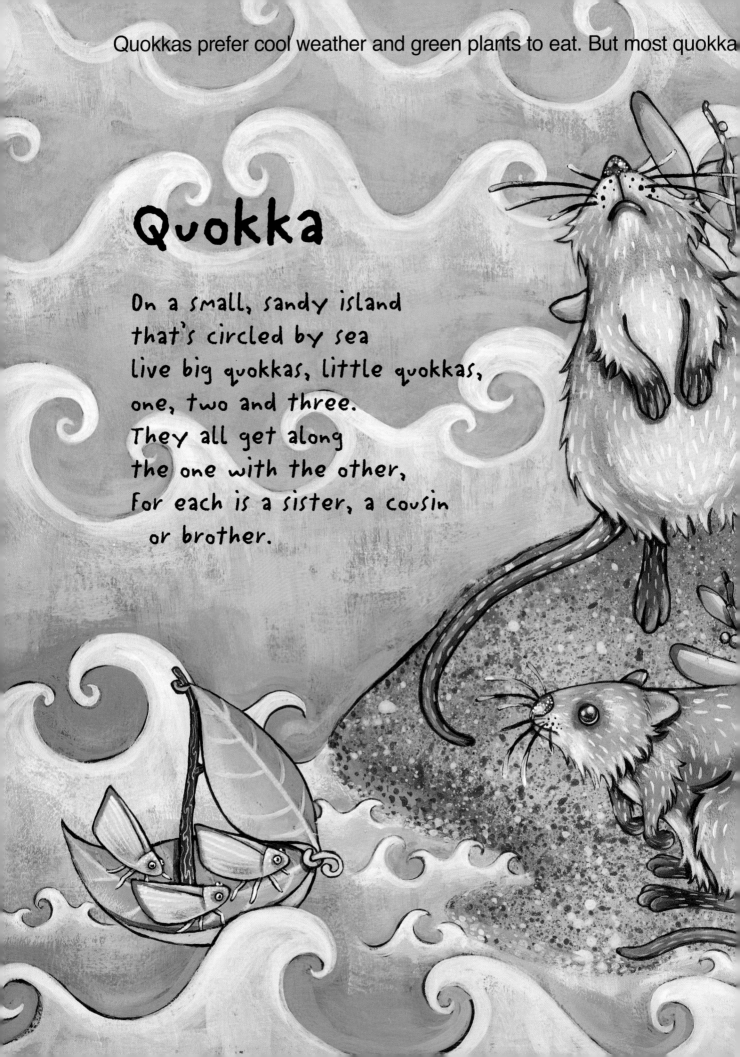

Quokka

On a small, sandy island
that's circled by sea
live big quokkas, little quokkas,
one, two and three.
They all get along
the one with the other,
for each is a sister, a cousin
or brother.

ve on a sandy island called Rottnest Island. Plants grow there in winter, but summer is hot and dry. Quokkas carry their babies in a pouch.

Rabbit-eared bilbies have a long nose, long ears and silky fur. They also have a pouch to carry

Bilby

Bilby doesn't like to squat
on desert sand when it is hot.
So his burrow's cool and round,
nice and deep below the ground.

Emus are big, tall birds. They have small wings and feathers, but cannot fly. Emus eat insects and grass. They swallow stones to help digest their food.

Emu

Emu is a fattish mound
of feathers on two legs,
with fluffy, stripy babies
from largish, greenish eggs.
He also has two goggly eyes,
with which to peer and peek,
and is thought of,
as a sort of, nosy stickybeak!

eyes closed. A platypus uses the sense of touch to get around. It eats worms

A platypus has fur, a large tail and a flat, tough bill. It sees and hears well, but swims with its

Platypus

It doesn't matter, platypus,
that you're a funny mix-up—
you're rarely seen
in rivers green,
for nothing of you sticks up!

a long, deep burrow. Wombats come out to eat at night. They eat tree roots

A wombat is a big animal. It has fur, short legs, a tail and a blunt snout. It uses its claws to make

Wombat

She mightn't look sleek
and when on her feet
she rocks side-to-side as
 she strolls.
But she's slow and she's steady
and ever so ready
to dig and to burrow in holes.

Pet galahs can be taught to 'talk' — but they don't understand!

Galahs are cockatoos. They fly in big flocks.

Galah

Hooray! Hoorah!
The pink galah
is an acrobatic circus star!
Above the ground, upside down,
a whirling, twirling, crazy clown.
He sets off such a brouhaha —
cheeky, beaky, silly galah!

Pelicans are large flying birds. They live in rivers or lakes. They dip their long bill and pouch into shallow water to catch fish.

Pelican

A pelican likes to swim about
and fill his beak with fishes.
That shows he's clever —
for he never
needs to think of dishes.

enemy, they raise their frill and hiss. They can grow up to one metre long

Frill-necked lizards have a flat frill around their neck. If they are angry or want to scare away an

Frill-necked lizard

It's lucky that lizard isn't vain
with mirrors about the place —
I'm sure he wouldn't like it much
if he could see his face.
For when this lizard's frightened
he lifts his frill and spits,
and if he saw just how he looked
he'd scare himself to bits!

Kangaroo

The bound-along roo, as you may know,
has a tail she's awfully keen on.
If it wasn't as long
and wasn't as strong,
what would she possibly lean on?

balance when hopping or to lean on when they are resting. Kangaroo babies are called joeys. Joeys crawl into the mother's pouch to feed. Kangaroos eat grasses and other plants.

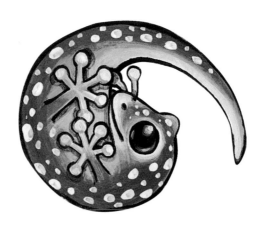